48 Hours
to a
Stronger Marriage

48
Hours
to a
Stronger
Marriage

*Reconnect with Your Spouse
and Re-energize Your Marriage*

BOB BOWERSOX

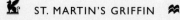 ST. MARTIN'S GRIFFIN ⚶ NEW YORK

Library of Congress Cataloging-in-Publication Data

Bowersox, Bob.
    48 hours to a stronger marriage: reconnect with your spouse and
    re-energize your marriage / Bob Bowersox.—1st ed.
        p. cm.
    ISBN 0-312-28114-5
    1. Marriage. 2. Communication in marriage. I. Title: Forty-
eight hours to a stronger marriage. II. Title.

HQ734 .B7593 2002
306.81—dc21   2001048879

First Edition: February 2002

10 9 8 7 6 5 4 3 2 1

To Toni and Taylor,
for us

CONTENTS

ACKNOWLEDGMENTS

First and foremost, I want to thank my wife and partner, Toni Ann Parisi Bowersox, for her strength and tenacity in her constant efforts to improve our life together. Toni, I am convinced that your senses of relationship, of family— of simply being together—will, in the end, prove to be our rock. I'm so glad you're in my life. Thanks for all your wise counsel with Reacquaintance.

And speaking of wise counsel—I owe an enormous debt to my friend and agent, Liza Dawson. Thanks, Liza, for seeing the possibilities in my simple idea and for making the effort to find the right home for it.

And boundless thanks to Leslie Garisto, whose wonderful talent with the written word smoothed all the rough edges. Couldn't have done it as well without you, Leslie.

And thanks to Scott Manning for all his help getting the word out.

Thanks also to Bernard G. Guerney Jr., whose work and book helped open my eyes and suggest some tools that actually work.

And finally, thanks to all my new friends at St. Martin's Press: my editor, Elizabeth Beier, for her openness, acceptance, and immediate enthusiasm for the book; Michael Connor for his help and expertise in editing; and Matthew Shear for the opportunity.

FOREWORD
by David I. Mandelbaum, Ph.D.

In over twenty years as a practicing psychotherapist specializing in working with adolescents, couples, and families, my approach to helping patients with their relationships has been influenced by two assumptions that I've confirmed time and again.

The first is that all relationships are affected by cultural myths and stereotypes—fictions that usually have little to do with the real-world relationship. One myth, promoted by popular media, is that once you meet the partner of your dreams, he or she will be sufficient to meet all your relationship needs, and that those needs will be constant and enduring. The reality, however, is that individuals change over time. As they do so, their requirements need to be satisfied in different ways.

The second assumption is that we are expected to know or intuit the skills required to make a relationship work over time. It seems to be expected that couples should know how to tap into their own needs, to express them with compassion, and to listen with empathy to their partner's needs—all skills that have been shown to predict success and contentment in relationships. But the reality is that many of us simply don't naturally know how to behave this way.

Many of us tend to accept these myths without question. Paired with a lack of skills about relationship development and maintenance, pervasive myths contribute to the frustration, disappointment, and resentment that many people in long-term relationships begin to feel. It's uncommon for us to intuitively understand how people—and therefore relationships—change. Nor do we know how to clearly share with our significant other how things are changing in ourselves or to listen to *them* about the changes they are experiencing.

In this elegantly simple yet profoundly important book, Bob Bowersox has developed an approach that goes a long way toward solving the difficulties I've pinpointed above. First, he has developed an intriguing, structured questionnaire, which he calls "The Form for Reacquaintance," that promises to help individuals accomplish a very important goal: to become more clearly aware of one's own values, priorities, and beliefs about many aspects of the individual's personal needs. Implicit in "The Form for Reacquaintance" is the assumption that these beliefs and values have evolved over the course of the relationship; but because they haven't typically been shared (a requirement for intimacy and relationship satisfaction), many couples have slowly drifted apart, feeling increasingly disconnected and frustrated.

Second, Bowersox proposes a way to exchange information that encourages openness and increased sharing of these needs between relationship partners. Bob's easy-to-follow guidelines will help readers learn to speak interactively and listen empathetically. My experience shows that these skills increase intimacy and satisfaction with and within a relationship.

If you follow the suggestions Bob offers in the book, you can expect increased self-awareness, increased relationship skill development, and, most importantly, increased knowledge of and intimacy with your significant other. I predict that those who follow the suggestions in this book will learn more about their partners and will develop a more open and loving relationship based upon who one's partner *really* is rather than on a projected fantasy.

While this book was written for nonprofessionals and is

easy and fun for couples to use on their own, I have found the questionnaire extremely helpful in my own professional practice. It has provided a structure that has enabled the couples I work with to learn far more about each other in a more efficient manner than in traditional couples work. Couples therapists will find this book extremely useful in making their own work more efficient.

On a more personal note, my wife and I enjoyed a Reacquaintance experience, as described in Bob's book, and were both surprised at the level of knowledge we didn't have about each other after more than ten years of marriage. Going through "The Form for Reacquaintance" using the suggested guidelines increased our self-awareness, our awareness of each other, and the intimacy we felt as a couple. This book was very helpful to us, a couple who have been actively committed to developing a continuing intimate relationship.

For couples who are less familiar with the concepts and techniques in this book than I was as a practicing couples psychotherapist, the experience of Reacquaintance actually may prove to be a savior.

48 Hours
to a
Stronger Marriage

1

MY STORY—AND YOURS

For she and I were long acquainted
And I knew all her ways.
—A. E. HOUSMAN, "FANCY'S KNELL"

We must never assume that which is incapable of proof.
—G. H. LEWES

THIS BOOK IS A LOVE STORY. It begins on the day that I first met Toni Parisi, the woman who would become my wife, my lover, my helpmate, and the mother of my daughter, Taylor. Like all good love stories, it's a tale of romance and passion and devotion. And like every relationship grounded in reality, it's also a story of deadlines and housework and family obligations—all those everyday duties that whittle away at romance and, as I discovered when it was almost too late, keep us from genuinely knowing the person we've chosen to spend our life with.

If you're reading this with more than a passing interest, I suspect it's your story as well, which turns out to be a very good thing because this is a love story with a happy ending. It's not a fairy tale, mind you. It took me months of soul-searching and hours of research, with not a fairy godmother in sight, to come up with the solution—Reacquaintance—that forms the core of this book. And there really isn't an ending per se: Reacquaintance, as it turns out, is an ongoing, lifelong process, a continuum of discovery and rediscovery. As you read on and move through the process yourself, I think you'll find it every bit as exciting in its own way as those heady, falling-in-love days. And I hope you'll come to believe, as I do, that love isn't a one-shot deal but our most precious renewable resource.

When Things Were Right

I fell in love with Toni on July 5, 1984, at 9:30 P.M.—though I didn't know it at the time. The night was hot and humid, and I was standing with my chums Bill and Mitch on the upper level of the back-deck bar of the Rusty Rudder in Dewey Beach, Delaware, watching the last wash of pink and gold drain from the sky. The place was packed and noisy; a three-piece band was playing techno-pop dance music. Citronella candles burned on the heavy, wood-plank tables. I felt terrific.

Bill, Mitch, and I were the Three Musketeers that summer, a trio of good-looking, professional, single guys in search of all the things single guys search for. We were doing well, producing film soundtracks, commercials, and a nationally syndicated radio show. We'd rented a swank condo at the beach, and by the July Fourth weekend we were wired into every aspect of the beach scene and much appreciated by the local bartenders. Our evenings usually began at the Rudder, on that upper-level deck near the table that was reserved, every evening, in our names.

True to form I was standing near the table with my back to the deck, listening to the music and hoping the wind blowing off the Rehoboth Bay would ease the humidity a bit. I felt a tap on my shoulder—Mitch, gesturing toward the door.

"Look who just walked in," he said.

I looked across the deck, and there was Phyllis Dorn. A longtime friend, Phyllis was gorgeous, intelligent, lots of fun. It was always good to see Phyllis. And then I looked just past her, across sixty feet of deck, and my whole life changed.

Standing next to Phyllis was her best friend, Toni. Petite, slim, beautiful, in a white halter top and pink shorts, her smile radiant, her face serene as if the heat and humidity couldn't touch her (How do women do that?). She turned and looked directly at me. And that's the image I remember of Toni, still clear in my mind more than seventeen years later. The rest of the evening is a mosaic of random, unfocused images. But Toni at sixty feet—that's still as clear and sharp as the facets of a diamond.

We started dating regularly, usually long dinners in quiet restaurants. We'd spend the entire time talking, like we had to catch up on the past thirty years in four short hours. We shared anything and everything; we wanted to learn all there was to know about each other. I don't think we were any different from most couples. You probably experienced something similar with your partner—a hunger for each other that's only satisfied by being together and learning as much as you possibly can about each other.

Toni and I were a pretty good match—not identical spirits, but complementary, like two pieces of a puzzle. At the time we met, she was a professional lighting designer with a great sense of taste and a natural artistic gift. She was practical and grounded, soft-spoken but direct, and very much nonconfrontational (though occasionally, her Italian passion would flare up in defense of something she really believed in). I, on the other hand, was a dreamer, passionate about everything to a fault. I believed (and still do) that anything is possible, and I've never let practical considerations stop me from trying, even against overwhelming odds. Over the years I've helped Toni dream, and she's kept me realistic.

Four years after that night at the Rusty Rudder, we were married in a sunny outdoor ceremony full of flowers and friends. We spent two weeks laughing and loving on an idyllic Caribbean island then settled into building our life together. Professional success came quickly for both of us, Toni's in the lighting field and mine as on-camera talent for electronic retailing giant QVC, and acting in film and TV. But even though we were busy, we still found time for those long, candlelit, conversation-filled dinners. Our relationship was vibrant and enriching.

Two years after our wedding day, our daughter, Taylor, was born, the capstone blessing of the marriage. Toni decided to leave the working world to be a full-time mom, something we both agreed was important. At about that same time, my career at QVC went into hyperdrive as American consumers opened their arms to electronic retailing. Suddenly I was traveling more, away from home as much as six days at a stretch. Toni began to fill some of her free time with charity work, getting involved with the Delaware Epilepsy Foundation and eventually being elected to its board of directors. She also went back to college to earn her degree in education.

Life was good but busy, our schedules overflowing with work and classes, travel and personal appearances, pre-school obligations and visits to the pediatrician. There was less and less time for those candlelit dinners. But we were okay: Secure in our love for each other, we had faith that eventually things would slow down, even out, get back to normal. Life, as I said, was good, so how could anything be wrong?

But something *was* wrong. Only four years into our marriage, and we sensed something shifting in the undercurrents of our relationship, though neither Toni nor I could pinpoint exactly what it was. On the surface we were as committed to the marriage as we'd always been. But we were beginning to feel out of sync: A comment made in jest—the sort of thing that would once have resulted in a game of clever repartee—would draw, instead, a short, angry retort. An offhand observation would be taken as a

personal shot across the bow. Personality quirks, once en-
dearing, were suddenly "things to work on." Gifts bought
with certainty were received with something less than enthusiasm.

I began to notice that little things Toni did seemed
somehow out of character. Apparently she was noticing the
same about me. And the fire we'd once felt in each other's
presence didn't seem to be burning quite so fiercely. I re-
membered when I couldn't wait to get into the same air
as Toni, to talk about every detail of her day, every thought
that crossed her mind. Now it seemed like we were doing
it all in shorthand: a quick kiss on the cheek, a rushed,
"How was your day?" a *Reader's Digest* condensed rundown,
and then we'd be off into the part of our lives that we
thought really demanded our attention: work, child care,
financial obligations, overtime. The passions and certain-
ties of our marriage seemed to be evaporating, and we
couldn't figure out why.

Why Things Go Wrong

During the early years of our marriage, I developed a habit
of retiring upstairs three or four nights a week to write.
While I was working on my first novel, Toni would get
involved in projects of her own—painting, decorating, gardening, reading. I did worry that I was leaving her alone
too often, but when I asked her about it, she pooh-poohed
it, told me she was proud of me and that she felt comfortable just knowing I was in the house.

Two years after that, however, as I was getting into my
second novel, I began to sense a change in Toni, especially
on those nights when I'd excuse myself and head upstairs
to write. One night she'd seem a little down; another she'd
be short with me or altogether unresponsive. But we had
an understanding about the writing, didn't we?

Over several months, though, her displeasure became

more and more apparent. She stopped asking me about the novel's progress, and she was increasingly quiet and withdrawn, but with a hair trigger. One night the mounting tension erupted into an argument, and a pretty caustic one at that. We were sufficiently shaken by it to sit down and try to figure out, finally, what was going on. And we began to realize that, just beyond our awareness, lots of things in our life had changed. QVC's demands on my time had quadrupled, forcing me to commit more and more energy and focus there. I was also in greater demand as an actor. Toni, for her part, was the mother of a young child by that time, the toughest and most time-consuming job on the planet and—if your partner is busy elsewhere—the loneliest as well.

It became clear that Toni needed more than just my presence in the house. Without realizing it she had started to read my leaving her to write as a tacit rejection—the writing was more important than her. We spent most of that evening talking things out, and we began to understand that certain fundamental things about us had changed. Without that soul-searching conversation, we might have misread the argument as evidence of the fact that we were growing apart. In reality, though, Toni had been growing closer to me in her feelings, longing for the togetherness of the early days of our relationship.

Getting Back to Right

That argument, and our subsequent conversation, put an end, once and for all, to the notion that things were fundamentally okay and would sort themselves out on their own. But knowing that something needed to be done and understanding how to do it are two very different things. I began to wonder what else about Toni might have changed in the last eight years. And what about me? Was

I really the same easygoing guy who'd stood on the deck of the Rusty Rudder trawling for good times? Toni and I had built a home, pursued careers, become parents. What else about us—what beliefs, hopes, needs, and desires—had changed? I was suddenly aware that the woman I'd fallen in love with was, in many ways, not the woman I was currently in love with. What I'd understood about her then, or even a year ago, needed to be updated, and she needed to do the same with me.

But how do you do that? How do you determine what's changed in eight or ten years without taking another eight or ten years to go through it all? We knew we could talk about it, sure. And we tried to. But without some kind of structure or guidance, we'd end up sliding off focus, talking about the problems of the moment or the things that loomed on our To Do lists. And sometimes we'd end up arguing again, telling each other, "You don't understand what I'm dealing with," or, "It's always about you, isn't it?" Eventually, we sought the help of a therapist. But it felt unnatural to us, as though we were talking through the counselor and not directly to each other, as though the agenda were his and not our own.

So I began to read. I read all those books that traced my lineage to one planet and Toni's to another. They offered me valuable insights into men and women in general, but they didn't tell me a whole lot about the two of us as unique individuals with our own particular histories and problems. So I moved on, prowling the magazine racks, taking quiz after quiz (whose answers intrigued me) but, once again, seemed overly general. And then one night I had my epiphany.

I was doing some woodworking, of all things, trying to match two pieces of wood with different grains so that they appeared to be a single piece. Playfully, I imagined myself "introducing" the two pieces to each other. And then it occurred to me: The best way to acquaint yourself with someone is to introduce yourself. Or put more personally, the best way to *re*acquaint myself with Toni was to have her reintroduce her self-of-the-moment to me and for me to reintroduce my self-of-the-moment to her in turn.

Easy to say. But we needed some help—something that would allow us to bring all that new information together quickly and simply, while preserving the excitement of discovery and the adventure of sharing ourselves.

And so began the process that would eventually become this book. I developed my first Form for Reacquaintance, a series of questions designed to help Toni and me reveal the people we'd become. The Form covered just twenty-two topics at that time and dealt mostly with priorities of the moment, self-image and hopes and dreams. It included topics like "my three most secret desires," "my current biggest fear," and "two things I really need right now." I printed out two copies and gave one to Toni. We agreed to fill them in over the next few days, then meet at a restaurant to share our answers. The process of filling out the Form was simple and a lot of fun, and I liked the fact that it made me think about things that hadn't crossed my mind in a while, like what *was* most important to me at the moment, and what *would* I change about myself if I could. It also forced me to ask myself some questions I'd been putting off: What *were* my priorities? What *did* I hope to accomplish in the coming year?

And then came the dinner, each of us taking turns reading our response to a particular question. Without a doubt it was the most powerful, revealing, intimate, exciting, entertaining, amusing, and surprising experience I'd had with Toni in a decade. Aside from the things we said to each other, I don't remember anything else about that night—rather like the night we'd first met. It was as though I were meeting Toni for the first time and falling in love with her all over again.

What the Form Can Do for You

As we discovered that night, "The Form for Reacquaintance" can be a powerful tool. Reading and listening to the responses helped us gain enormous insight into each other; almost every answer was greeted with a, "Really?" or, "I had no idea." But the Form's true value, we saw, lay in the conversation it initiated—an amazing, revelatory talk about the things that had changed for each of us, why they'd changed, and the impact of those changes on our lives and on our marriage. We talked about things we hadn't discussed in years with an intimacy that startled and moved us.

Since that extraordinary day, "The Form for Reacquaintance" has grown and diversified. I've added dozens of topics and delved into a host of new areas. I've added questions on work, home and family matters, artistic and social topics, relationships and intimacy. I've expanded the questions dealing with beliefs, philosophies, and emotional needs, because these are the core areas that really affect the way we act and react. Like the people who fill it out, the Form will undoubtedly continue to evolve. As you and your partner use it over time—and it's meant to be used time and again—new questions will almost certainly occur to you both (I've included a special fill-in section for just such topics).

It's my hope that "The Form for Reacquaintance" will serve as a starting point for you, initiating a conversation that will go on through all the years you're together. I hope you'll continue to use the Form to strengthen and refresh your partnership, add to the depth of your understanding of each other, and intensify your feelings for each other.

That way the next time someone asks you when you met, you can reply, "The first time? Or the last time?"

2

DO I REALLY KNOW WHAT
I THINK I KNOW?

> . . . human expectation
> is that love remains the same.
> —PAUL SIMON, "YOU'RE THE ONE"

IF I WERE TO ASK YOU WHY you picked up this book, what would you say? What was it about the title that made you stop, lift it from the shelf, and take a look inside?

I'd guess it was more than idle curiosity. In fact, I'd be willing to wager that, for the briefest of instants, the part of you that can't lie to yourself clearly felt something. A shock of recognition, maybe, felt in the back of your heart, the realization that a gulf exists between what you hoped your relationship would be by this time and what you honestly, deep down, know it has become—or is becoming.

I'd also guess that what moved you was the hope for a stronger, more vibrant connection with your partner, but you haven't a clue as to how to get there. I know. I felt the same things not all that long ago. And instead of looking for a way to make things right, I rationalized. Sure, I told myself, the relationship isn't what it was in the beginning, but it's basically okay, isn't it?

No. It wasn't for me, and it isn't for you. That's why you picked up this book. In that part of you that can't lie, you know that something's changed. And change is scary. It's also inevitable and—as you'll discover as you read on—an incredibly powerful and positive force.

Change Happens

There's no stopping change, and there's no escaping it. Look around you, and you can't miss it. Even granite is worn down eventually, altered by wind and water and the accumulated steps of passing strangers, until what was once solid is now sand. Human beings change, too, physically and emotionally. Our cells are continually renewing themselves, and those new cells are acted upon by the environment and our culture in ways large and small, so that physically we're not the same people we were even yesterday, and we're *markedly* different from the people we were a decade ago.

The same is true of our emotional selves. Our priorities, motivations, inner support mechanisms, likes and dislikes evolve and mutate every bit as much as our bodies do. The person you were last year, not to mention ten years ago, responded to a different set of assumptions, reacted against very different fears, was impelled by very different hopes and desires than the person you are now. Yet most of these changes have been subtle, and cumulative, so that you barely noticed them on a day-to-day basis.

If change is happening to you, of course, it's happening to your partner as well. But if we have trouble keeping up with the alterations in ourselves, how can we expect to recognize change in someone else—even someone we profess to love, someone we've spent years with?

The fact is that, quite often, we can't. In spite of the evidence all around us, we doggedly believe that the person we greet every morning over orange juice is the same person we'd breathlessly embraced when we were falling in love. And we compound this mistake by expecting—and insisting—that this essentially "new" person act and respond as the person he or she was one, two, three years ago or more. When our expectations are thwarted, we feel confused, hurt, and angry. We feel out of touch with the one person we always felt would understand and accept us. We don't understand why that person we love seems to be less responsive and disconnected. Or we simply wonder why things don't feel "right."

I use the word "we" because this inability to register change is a universal human phenomenon. In fact, recent groundbreaking research is revealing the surprising truth that most of us don't really know what we think we know about our partners. And it's exactly that lack of knowledge that leads to the sense of loss we feel as a relationship matures. In the worst case, it can even contribute to the destruction of the relationship.

The Intimacy Gap

When you look at your partner over a candlelit dinner or the morning newspaper, do you really know the person you're sitting with? Can you say that you're truly confident in your knowledge of that person? Most of us would answer both questions with an unequivocal "Yes." And most would be wrong. Because, in fact, the longer we stay together, the more we *think* we know but the less accurate that information really is. And as we go about our lives together, an Intimacy Gap opens between us without our knowing it.

Blame it on the faulty way we gather information about each other. Or, more to the point, blame it on our failure to update that information over time. You see, in the early days of a relationship, we absorb an extraordinary amount of data about one another. Things like aspirations, fears, what we'd rescue in a fire, our favorite way of making love—everything from our image of God to our favorite movie. And as the relationship flowers and grows, we learn more, "meeting" each other a piece at a time. Fragment by fragment, layer upon layer, we absorb information about each other; and gradually, we get a sense of who this person we've fallen in love with really is. In the early days of a relationship, we can't get enough of each other; in fact, it's the learning about each other that fuels the passion. But in the midst of all this learning, we begin to make our first real mistake. We assume that the things we've learned about this wonderful, sensuous, intelligent person we've fallen in love with are set in stone. And we gradually stop pursuing the learning and fall into a routine of relating based on the information we've absorbed.

What we don't anticipate is that there will be changes—lots of them—in every facet of our lives. We can't imagine that the person we fell in love with on that first evening isn't the person we'll sleep next to tonight or glance at between meetings five years down the line. But much of who that lover of ours was one, two, ten years ago has evolved—maybe only slightly, maybe a lot. And the trouble is that most of us fail to register those changes. We continue to relate to them based upon obsolete information gathered years ago. And that lack of corrected knowledge—that Intimacy Gap—can cause some serious problems.

I learned this painfully through personal experience. But a pair of researchers at the University of Texas at Austin have proven it through clinical observation. And what they discovered goes a long way toward explaining the Intimacy Gap I've been referring to.

Confidence Versus Accuracy

In 1997, William B. Swann Jr. and Michael J. Gill, two psychological researchers at the University of Texas at Austin, undertook a series of studies designed to look into what couples knew about each other and what they thought about what they knew. Their conclusions amounted to a revelation in the psychology of relationships.[1]

Put simply, Swann and Gill determined that the longer we stay together, the more we think we know about each other but the less accurate that information is. Even more importantly, they concluded that "people's lack of insight into the accuracy of their beliefs could cause them to base important decisions on erroneous but confidently held beliefs," and that "confidence-accuracy dissociations may also lead to disharmony in relationships."

In other words, what you think you know, you don't; and what you don't know can cause a lot of trouble in your relationship.

To get at that astonishing information, Swann and Gill began by recruiting eighty random couples through a University of Texas newspaper ad and inviting the participation of dating students enrolled in an introductory psychology course. On the day of the study, they randomly assigned one member of each couple to a role they called "Target," and the other to a role they called "Perceiver."

The Targets were given several questionnaires to answer in which they were asked to rate themselves in various aspects of their lives, including how they viewed themselves with respect to self-esteem, self-liking, personal competence, social competence, intelligence, artistic and musical ability, athleticism, attractiveness, sexual behavior, and so on.

Perceivers were given the same questionnaire, but with one important difference: They were instructed to answer each question "the way you *think your partner would answer.*" Perceivers also had to rate—on a scale of 0–100 percent—how confident they were that they *accurately* predicted their partner's response to each item.

Finally, both Targets and Perceivers separately answered questions about their relationship itself—how long it had lasted, how long they would want it to last, how much they loved their partner, and how they felt their relationship compared to their imagined ideal.

Of all the surprising results of the study, what was most surprising to the two researchers was how *overconfident* the Perceivers were about what they knew. Most of the time, the Perceivers thought they were answering the questions just as their partners would. But most of the time, they were dead wrong. Suddenly, a relatively simple study got a lot more complex. What is the relationship between confidence in what we think we know and the accuracy of that knowledge? Why, Swann and Gill wondered, are people so woefully overconfident about what they think they know about their partners and, most of the time, so astonishingly wrong? And why is the discrepancy so dangerous?

As I began to suspect from my own research, it has everything to do with the way we gather information about each other. As we become increasingly intimate—as our relationship develops—we hunger for knowledge about our partner. We eagerly pursue it. And because we *really like* this person, we're motivated to build a bank of impressions about them as quickly as possible. The more time we spend with this magnetic other, the richer the bank of impressions, and the richer the impressions, the more confident we become in them. But as Swann and Gill discovered, this confidence is misplaced pretty much from day one.

But how can that be?

Well, it turns out that there are two types of data we take in about our partner, what Swann and Gill called "diagnostic" and "nondiagnostic" information. Diagnostic information is Sgt. Joe Friday's, "Just the facts, ma'am":

things like the color of your lover's hair (say, brown), her job (physician's assistant, for example), his daily workout (jogging). These are known, indisputable facts.

Nondiagnostic information is more nebulous; it derives from the *assumptions* we make *based* on the facts we've gathered: I *assume* she's a physician's assistant *because she wants to be a doctor. I figure* he jogs *because he's afraid of a heart attack.*

It's the nondiagnostic information, of course, that starts to blur the picture. Swann and Gill explained it this way: "Although rich representations of others may foster confidence, they will not necessarily contribute to accuracy."[2]

In other words, having lots of information about someone we love gives us the impression that we know them, though that impression isn't necessarily correct. Or, in the researcher's words:

> The problem is that nondiagnostic information may contribute to richness just as much as diagnostic information. For example, learning that one's relationship partner has certain qualities (e.g., "gives to charity," "exudes innocence," "is a regular churchgoer") could make one more confident of an objectively unrelated quality (e.g., "has not had many sexual partners") if one . . . erroneously assumes that all such qualities are expressions of "morality." In such instances, nondiagnostic information will foster richness and confidence, but not accuracy.[3]

From the beginning, we weave a mental tapestry of our partner, some of it based on truth and much of it based on assumptions. The more detailed the tapestry, the more likely we are to feel confident that we truly know the other person—though in fact, many of the details are entirely of our own creation. This being true, Swann and

Gill concluded that "as the amount of time and involvement in a relationship increase, people's impressions may become increasingly confident, but no more accurate. They may thus develop an illusory feeling of knowing their partner."[4]

This is exactly the Intimacy Gap I spoke about earlier. And as the research has revealed, it doesn't matter how long you've been together. In fact, Swann and Gill found that after that first heady time of getting to know each other—the infatuation period, if you will—the accuracy about our early impressions and those that follow and build upon the first increase very little. We tend to stick with what we first learned about our partner, even while our partner subtly—and sometimes not so subtly—moves on, learns, grows, and changes. Despite all common sense, despite evidence to the contrary, we doggedly continue to hold on to the conviction that what we know about the person we love is accurate. The discrepancy between confidence and accuracy—the Intimacy Gap— opens, and grows larger, like one road diverging into two and the two getting increasingly farther apart but staying in sight of each other. And in spite of the divergence, we continue as we always have, believing that things are perfectly okay.

Of course they're not. Like those roads, we're moving farther and farther away from each other. We sense it, but because we appear to be close—sharing a bed, a kitchen, a schedule, a set of household and perhaps parental duties—we refuse to believe it. We continue to relate to our partner in a consistent way based upon the knowledge we have and believe to be accurate. And based upon that belief, *we gradually stop pursuing the learning—the very thing that fueled the original passion—and we assume we know most of what there is to know regarding our lover.* We stop the pursuit; we fall out of love and fall into routine; and we begin to sense that things are askew. We long for things to be better. We're stuck.

So What Do We Do?

We get reacquainted.

3

THE CONCEPT OF REACQUAINTANCE

ac·quaint (*vt*) **1** : to cause to know personally **2** : to make familiar : cause to know firsthand

re- (*prefix*) **1** : again : anew
—WEBSTER'S NEW COLLEGIATE DICTIONARY, 1981

THE IDEA THAT WE MIGHT not know our lover as well as we thought we did is an unsettling one. It not only makes us question what we really know about our partner, but we question ourselves as well. How could we have missed so much? We thought we were paying attention and totally involved here. What happened?

Even more unsettling is not having a clue as to how to turn things around, how to bring those two diverging roads back together. Once we accept the fact that a lot has changed so subtly that we didn't even notice it, how do we go about learning what those changes were—what's evolved, what old has been dropped, what new has been added? How do we catch up on three, five, ten, or fifteen years of those subtle changes in ourselves and our partners?

I began to suspect that there might be a lot of couples like Toni and me who'd grown out of touch on the fundamentals of each other as individuals, who'd misplaced that deep connectedness and intimacy we were immersed in when first learning about each other—couples like us who couldn't seem to get off the surface of things anymore.

Oh, we had the "partnership" of our relationship down by this time—*this* was *her* responsibility, *that* was *mine*, *these* we shared.

And we were great at the "couple's small talk," too. Does this sound familiar?

"How was *your* day?"
"OK, I guess. Did the shopping. Did the wash. What happened with *you* today?"
"Same old, same old. Kids home?"
"Yeah, they're upstairs."
"What's for dinner?"
"Kids want pizza."
"OK with me. Hey, did you hear about Jack?" . . .

Relationship Shorthand 101, right? Quick, to the point, the semblance of meaningful communication. Yeah, our *marriage* was working great, no doubt about it. But we hadn't fallen in love with a *marriage*. We'd fallen in love with a *person*. Were we seeing that person anymore? And if we did see someone there, were we sure we knew who that person was *now?* What was important to them *now?* Were we relating to *them* now or an *image* of *them* that we held in our mind and memory, an image pieced together years ago from information that was valid *then?*

Everything we'd learned about each other had been dutifully filed away, locked in place, and was now serving as the database we referred to whenever we wanted to determine what to expect from our mate in regard to anything, from what he or she thought about their work to what our mate liked most about our lovemaking. We'd become so certain of what we thought we knew that we didn't think about it anymore. We reacted automatically, based on old information. We accepted that "routine of relating."

But now I had an inkling of the problem. I realized that what Toni and I knew about each other might not be accurate anymore. We needed to update. But how to do it effectively and at the same time make the process of discovering each other again as exciting and adventurous as it had been the first time?

The Form for Reacquaintance

In its earliest incarnation, "The Form for Reacquaintance" was designed to help two specific people—my wife and me—reintroduce ourselves to each other. I saw the concept of Reacquaintance as a simple, pleasurable way for us to bring each other into focus again—to update ourselves, if you will. Meeting Toni had been the most thrilling event of my life. I wanted to meet her again, learn about her again, fall in love with her again.

And I did. The Form and the process worked just as I'd hoped. But would it work for others as well as it had for us? To find out, I needed to recruit some willing participants. While not all were unequivocally thrilled about the idea of Reacquaintance before they participated, everybody felt that it had made a significant difference in the way they related after they'd gone through it. Among these couples, I've chosen several whose stories seemed to me worth sharing, not because they represented some universal relationship, but, in fact, because they formed a fairly diverse group, chronologically, geographically, socially, and culturally. And yet, in spite of the differences, there *were* certain universals—the sense that things could be better, the yearning (sometimes secret and unexpressed) for a deeper, more meaningful relationship, and after Reacquaintance, a sense of exhilaration and renewal. As you read through their stories, I hope you'll recognize a little bit of yourself and your partner in all of them. And I hope that their responses—starting below and continuing throughout the book—will offer up some emotional cheerleading, encouraging you to persevere in what could be the most exciting experiment of your marriage.

Beth and Rob

A pair of mutual friends decided that Beth and Rob were perfect for each other and colluded to get the two together. That was twenty-five years ago. This year the couple celebrated their twentieth anniversary and the ninth birthday of their daughter, Elly. "On the surface," says Beth, "we were very different people: Rob came from a working-class family and had had a strict Catholic upbringing; my parents were artists and very bohemian." But when Rob and Beth got to know each other, "the differences just melted away," says Beth. "I felt I could be perfectly honest with Rob. I could lay myself bare in an emotional sense, and not feel vulnerable—something that had never happened to me before."

> Resisting the temptation to send a message in my answers on the Form was a very positive experience for me. It was rougher than I'd thought. I guess I've been carrying around a whole lot of grudges I haven't owned up to.
>
> *—Beth*

At some point when she wasn't looking, though, that sense of trust began to erode. And as it did, without realizing it, Beth began to distance herself from Rob. "She insisted that she still loved me, and I guess I believed her," says Rob. "But we knew things weren't the same."

Both were anxious about the Reacquaintance process. "I

was afraid of revealing too much," says Beth, a fear Rob shared. Yet it was the very act of making themselves vulnerable again that allowed them to reconnect. The experience offered some genuine surprises: Beth, for instance, was astonished to discover that, in spite of being happy in his current job as a computer systems analyst, Rob had always regretted giving up a career in music. "I honestly thought he'd put it behind him years ago," she says. For his last birthday, Beth bought him an acoustic guitar. And now he's teaching her to play.

Don and Paula

Ironically, failed relationships brought Don and Paula together. They met in their forties after each had been through a painful divorce. "We were older and more practical by the time our relationship started," says Don. "But we talked a lot back then, especially about our lives and how we'd dealt with things up until that point." They married and had a child—a daughter, now ten. Both pride themselves in having no illusions about relationships and their volatility, but both are optimistic about their own marriage.

Interestingly, Reacquaintance reaffirmed a lot of what they felt they knew about each other. It also offered some startling realizations. "The little surprises—boy!" says Paula. "You may think you completely know yourself or your partner, but let me tell you—as much as you know, there's more that you don't."

Dick and Darlene

Work was the glue that cemented this May-December marriage. Dick and Darlene were coworkers when they met eighteen years ago; she was in her early twenties, and he was in his late forties. Not long after, they became partners in a dual sense, marrying and forming their own company. They have no children, but both have had to deal with a variety of medical problems over the last several years—a situation that's put some strain on their relationship. But Reacquaintance helped both of them with some personal healing. "I was so unaware of the fear Dick was hiding regarding my illness," says Darlene. "He always seemed so strong about it while I went through it, but during Reacquaintance, the emotions just poured out. I had no idea."

Reacquaintance taught them a great deal about each other, but most important, it offered them a whole new template for communication. "I seldom sit and listen," Dick admits. "In fact, we're both so used to talking—all the time, at the same time." Both were thrilled to discover that they could take turns speaking and listening, and they've made a conscious decision to change the way they communicate.

Nick and Andi

Financially successful, Nick and Andi have been together for seventeen years, thirteen of them as a married couple. He's a salesman for an international company and travels frequently. She's a teacher and homemaker. They have one daughter, who was born with physical and learning disabilities. And because they were so committed to helping their child, they inadvertently stopped focusing on each other. "We've been emotionally whipsawed back and forth because of our child and her needs," says Andi. "It's no wonder we've lost touch." Nick is even more frank: "Andi could have become a Buddhist, and I don't think I would have known," he admits.

The questions about family hit home for me. They really helped solidify how I felt about that area of my life and what had changed there for me. A lot of it Nick and I had nibbled around the edges of in discussions—or more accurately, arguments—but the Form really helped me zero in on what was important, so that when we talked about it later, I was very clear on it, very positive.

—Andi

I was stunned how much about myself I was consciously unaware of—little things you go through your days without considering. Filling out the Form brought so much of me out of the dark. When I was finished, I felt focused and defined, with a new sense of myself that I loved. I felt so much better about *me*. I remember thinking, how could I not be more impressive to Andi?

—Nick

Interestingly, Nick describes his reaction to Reacquaintance in physical terms: "It was like the electric current got turned on again," he says. For Andi, on the other hand, the most important effect of the process was a new sense of empathy. "It brought out compassion in both of us," she says, "that sense of being in the other person's shoes." She discovered that she'd been looking to Nick to solve all her problems and feeling angry with him when he couldn't— "or wouldn't, as I thought," she adds. "And then during Reacquaintance, I hear that he's struggling to make his life work, carrying the same kinds of burdens, with the same kinds of fears and needs. I really got a sense of 'We're in this together, partner.'"

Liz and Karl

Together for thirty-four years, Liz and Karl met in college and married after graduation. Today they live in Colorado, where Karl is a medical researcher in a cardiopulmonary lab. After a successful career in the fashion industry, Liz decided to go back to school and earn a second degree. She attends classes during the week and works part-time in a children's toy and book store. They have two grown children, a son who's pursuing a career in theater in New York City and a daughter who's returned home after a stay at a center for troubled youth.

> The Form drew more out of me than I'd expected. For instance, I'd originally thought that my personal goals should be much larger. But when I filled out the Form, I found myself writing about what seemed like small things. And I realized that before I hadn't been totally honest with myself. The Form helped me see that it really is the little things that make me happy.
>
> —*Liz*

Like many couples, they found themselves falling into a routine that didn't allow much room for romance or rediscovery. "You work all day, and you come home and you're beat, and you just want to kick back and watch the tube for a couple of hours or read or decompress," says Karl. "Where before you'd come home and all you'd want to do is spend more time one-on-one." And like so many couples, they discovered that the everyday demands of parenthood effected a sea change in their relationship. Even more damaging was the fact that their daughter had gone through some serious behavioral problems. "Despite our best efforts to hold things together in the marriage," says Karl, "it became very difficult."

Still, the marriage was "working," or so they assumed. Reacquaintance helped them see otherwise. "What's really interesting," says Karl, "is that we've been through so much professional counseling in the last few years because of our daughter and have already done so much work in this area as a couple and as a family. And yet we still came away from Reacquaintance with a tremendous amount." In addition to learning about Karl, Liz came away from the process with a new sense of herself. "It really helped me define some of my own goals," she says. "And now I feel like I can help Karl work toward the ones he wants. We're on the same pages together now."

The Form and What It Does

Like Liz, many of the participants told me that filling out "The Form for Reacquaintance" had helped them see things about themselves that had previously been hidden or unclear. I wasn't too surprised since the same thing had happened to Toni and me. This dual benefit, in fact, has been one of the pleasant surprises about the Form. By asking you to consider just who you are at the moment—your beliefs, hopes, fears, likes, and dislikes—it leads you on a path of self-discovery, which in turn leads you to the rediscovery of the person you love. But before this can happen, you have to understand what "The Form for Reacquaintance" is all about.

The Form is laid out in eight sections, each one dealing with a different part of your life. Part One, "Me," is designed to help you determine what you think of yourself in areas that include attractiveness, competence, artistic abilities, physical appearance, hopes, fears, needs, pet peeves, habits, and personal influences.

Part Two, "What's Important to Me," allows you to enumerate your priorities, your goals, and the things you hope to accomplish in widely divergent areas of your life.

Part Three, "What I Do," covers work and what you think of it, including current problems and goals. It also invites you to dream about time and money and what you'd do if you had more of both.

Part Four, "What I Believe," delves into matters both spiritual and philosophical.

Part Five, "My Relationships," helps you define your attitudes toward friendship and relationships.

Part Six, "Intimacies," is all about love—what you think about it, what you need from it, what turns you on physically and emotionally. It also helps you define your idea of romance and imagine a perfect romantic evening.

Part Seven, "Home and Family," addresses your feelings about your children, your partner, parenting, and home, and helps you determine what you cherish most about each.

Part Eight, "Things Specific to Us," will be a work in progress. It's a space for expanding and personalizing "The Form for Reacquaintance," much as Toni and I did during the early development of the Form. Here you can create topics and questions that can only be determined by you as a couple, specific to the two of you.

Each section of the Form contains several statements or questions that demand a specific response or set of responses from you. In formulating these responses, you take the first steps in the process of Reacquaintance: getting to know yourself a little better and preparing to share what you find with your partner.

Filling Out the Form

While the process of Reacquaintance is ultimately a shared experience, it actually begins with a solitary activity—the search for your most true and authentic self-of-the-moment. "The Form for Reacquaintance" will help you do just that. To help you fill out the Form, I've offered some guidelines below. And be sure to read "The Speaker," in chapter 5, which offers some advice on how to communicate your answers to your partner.

To start, you'll want to find a quiet, private place so that you can concentrate completely on the Form without any distractions. I've filled mine out in a different place each time—at the dining room table; alone in the house on a rainy afternoon with a couple of cups of tea; on the back porch on a sunny, crisp, fall afternoon; at a small desk tucked away in the corner of the local library. Choose a quiet place that makes you feel comfortable.

And give yourself sufficient time to reflect on each topic and your reactions to it—a couple of hours should do it. Some of these topics will test you. You'll have ambivalent feelings about them, or you'll need to dig down a little to find the right response. It's important not to feel rushed.

You don't want to be interrupted either. Find a place away from phones and pagers, kids in need of snacks or Band-Aids, neighbors dropping by to chat or borrow potting soil. Part of the beauty of the process is the sense of "the whole you" that evolves from filling out the Form in an uninterrupted flow. You'll find that the more focused you are when looking inward, the clearer the view becomes and the easier it will be to relate that view to your partner later. If your concentration is unbroken and your attention undiverted, you'll find that each section of the Form flows into the next with a kind of emotional logic, designed to help you determine the answer that's truest for you at this point in time.

Before you start, try to clear your mind of lingering distractions. This isn't the time to worry about tomorrow's meeting at work or what you need to pick up tonight for supper. As you proceed, be as honest with yourself as possible. And be aware that this honesty thing can be tricky.

Sometimes your brain might not want to hear what your heart is saying. I've discovered that it's often better to ask myself what I *feel* about something, rather than what I *think* about it. If you find yourself in a contest between heart and head, stick with the heart—it doesn't try to send messages or obscure truth. And don't discount your initial response: quite often it's the most emotionally honest. Give adequate thought to all your responses, but keep that first impression in mind while doing it. Finally, never forget that this is your chance to tell the person you love exactly who you are at the moment. You want this tapestry to be woven entirely of the truth.

Even more important than what you do while filling out the Form is what you don't do. Don't try to send messages with your answers. There's no tally here, and there's nothing to gain by trying to score a few subliminal points. For example, when you come to "Three areas I think our family needs work on" in Part Seven, resist the urge to make a list of Things That Bug Me About You. Your partner probably knows all about them already, and antagonism doesn't move the process forward.

Don't preach. You're not on a soapbox here. Personal views are required, but evangelism is not. Don't, for instance, try to convince your partner that the philosophical or spiritual views you revealed in Part Four are better than all others. Just state your beliefs and let your partner state his or hers. There'll be time later to return to any topic for further discussion if you desire.

Don't orate. Be as succinct as you can. Pare away the fat and deliver only the core of what you feel on any given subject. Most answers should be a phrase, or a sentence at most.

Don't use your responses to try to maneuver for an advantage on a hot subject between you. If you consider your spouse overly permissive with the kids, for instance, you may be tempted to list "lack of parental discipline" as a response to "My biggest worries about my children" in Part Seven. Don't. If you're worried that the kids seem a little wild, state that, and let the rest go for now.

Don't try to prove anything to your partner. This is an introduction, not a justification. You are what you are, and that's all you should be revealing. And don't try to prove anything to yourself either. Just fill in each blank with the truth for you as you know it at that moment.

Don't curtail your answers because they don't mesh with the realities of the moment. In Part Three, for example, you'll be asked to list "The kind of work I'd most like to do." If what you'd really like to do is become a pediatrician, then that's your answer, even if you haven't finished college and don't have a clue as to how you can pull it off. Who knows? If your partner understands that being a pediatrician is your heart's desire, maybe he or she can help you achieve it.

One last don't: Don't be afraid. Trust yourself and trust that the person you really are is the person your partner loves, that he or she *wants* to know this information about you, that he or she is hungry for it.

Finally, enjoy yourself. Half the fun of the Reacquaintance experience is meeting someone you haven't been in touch with for a while—yourself.

The other half, of course, is letting your partner in on the fun.

4

THE SETTING

A place for everything,
and everything in its place.
—SAMUEL SMILES, *THRIFT*

AS I LEARNED FROM MY OWN experiences with Reacquaintance, the setting you choose—and that includes both the time and the place—is a crucial element of the process. A good setting can make the difference between an experience that's smooth, comfortable, and pressure-free, and one that's disconnected, frustrating, and ultimately unsatisfying.

Once you and your partner have committed to the idea of Reacquaintance, you'll need to decide where and when you're going to become reacquainted. Optimally, you should give yourselves a minimum of forty-eight hours—forty-eight uninterrupted, you-and-you-alone-as-a-couple hours. You'll need to concentrate and focus and make a mutual commitment. So a little planning is required.

Pick a weekend or any two days in a row that are obligation-free. This should be a time when you can get away without anything hanging over your head or nagging at the back of your consciousness. If you have kids, choose a time when the grandparents or another couple can take them with a minimum of fuss and worry. This shouldn't be the weekend of the junior prom or the night before the big paper's due.

> We went the whole nine yards—took a weekend and went away to a nice hotel. It was wonderful to be pampered, to have anything we wanted just a call to the front desk away. We did Reacquaintance over a romantic dinner at one of our favorite restaurants, and we had the owner pick the menu for us, so all we had to concentrate on was each other (that was pretty cool to do just by itself). We booked a quiet corner table, and then we just went through the Forms. It couldn't have been better.
>
> —*Nick*

Some of us, wise as we are, still feel a pang of guilt when we head out on a child-free weekend. In fact, you can make this an adventure for your kids as well. Depending on their age, buy a few inexpensive toys and hide them around the house. Just before you leave, give each of the kids a treasure map with clues they'll have to figure out to lead them to each little "treasure" (for instance, hiding something behind the green living room couch can be "Your next treasure is waiting behind a large, green dragon that everyone sits on to watch TV"). I can vouch for the effectiveness of this technique since my parents consistently used it with my sister and me and it was always highly successful. It buffered the sting of their leaving and kept us occupied while they were gone. Keep in mind, too, that any benefit from Reacquaintance will be passed along to your kids. What child wouldn't choose two happy, loving parents over a pair of distant, unfulfilled harpies?

Clear the decks, work-wise. Don't leave anything hanging that you "just have to check on." This is a weekend for you and your partner, period. Leave the cell phone at home, stuff the pager in the sock drawer, tell the secretary you'll be unreachable. Forget about work, clubs, support groups. As you walk to the car, don't glance back at the laundry or the lawn. For two short days, commit all your time to each other. (Remember when you first met? You'd have given anything for the opportunity.) So dive in. Indulge only in yourselves.

> Just the fact that Nick was willing to focus on me so completely for two days did wonders for how I looked at us as a couple. I'd been getting to the point where I thought everything else in Nick's life was more important to him than me. But the hotel, and the dinner, his complete willingness to focus on me—it was like the first days of our relationship. A lot turned around for us right then and there.
>
> —*Andi*

And if you possibly can, get out of the house! You don't want to be interrupted by ringing phones or friends stopping by to chat or the UPS man asking you to sign for a package. You have only two obligations here—to reveal yourself and discover your partner. And you want to meet those obligations in a place that's serene, safe, and quiet.

> We did it over a nice, quiet dinner at home. Home is our favorite place, where we feel most comfortable. It's not hectic, and there are no obligations or hassles.
>
> —*Dick*

Need some ideas? Let me make a few suggestions:

Rent a cottage at the beach or in the mountains. Weekend rentals are often listed in the real estate section of the classifieds under "Real Estate—Rentals" or "Resort Real Estate." You can also contact real estate agents in the area you're traveling to; this is a good way to turn up a bargain or two for short rentals, especially in the off-season. And every resort area has one or two beautiful small hotels that would be perfect for a romantic weekend. If you can swing it, rent a suite or a luxury room. Go ahead, splurge. You'd have done it when you first met, right? Do it now.

Look in the yellow pages under "Bed-and-Breakfast" to locate a nearby romantic hideaway that you've been promising yourselves to try "one of these days." These days are here. Try to find one nestled away in the countryside where you can take long walks or sit and talk in a quiet, remote garden.

Check with the larger hotels in your area—many have two-day packages for incredibly low rates that often include Sunday breakfast in bed. There's nothing like spending two days being coddled and cosseted with the one you love, with room service and perhaps an oversized jacuzzi tub at your beck and call.

If you're near a major city on either coast, consider wrapping your Reacquaintance inside a four- or five-day cruise. Many cruise lines have short hops out and back—"cruises to nowhere"—that are perfect for a Reacquaintance experience. Stay away from the two- and three-day cruises though; these tend to be "party boats," with peace and quiet in short supply.

And then there are spas—marvelous resorts where you and your partner can indulge yourselves in glorious food, healing baths, exercise, and massage (not to mention a facial or a pedicure). These days you're likely to find several spas within driving distance of your home, wherever you live. And a spa offers you the possibility of physical as well as romantic renewal.

Outdoor types, on the other hand, might want to consider a nearby campground. Pitch a tent far from the madding crowd and experience your Reacquaintance bathed in the warmth of a romantic campfire.

What if, in spite of your best intentions and your fervent desires, you just can't get away? Rather than put off your Reacquaintance for another year or two, try a little creative subterfuge. Tell everyone you know that you're going away. Then stock the fridge, turn off the phone ringer, and ignore the doorbell. It's harder to do a focused, uninterrupted Reacquaintance at home, surrounded as you are by all the temptations of TV, hobbies, and housework, but it is possible to ignore them—unless, of course, they fit into your plan for Reacquaintance (*The Sopranos* by candlelight?).

Diverse as they are, all these locales share a common thread: Each in its way offers an environment conducive to togetherness. Remember, the Reacquaintance process is like a seed; to flourish and bear fruit, it needs a nurturing environment. And come to think of it, so do you. So take the time to carefully consider and plan your experience.

5

THE METHOD

Speak what we feel; not what we ought to say.
—WILLIAM SHAKESPEARE, *KING LEAR*

THERE ARE NEARLY AS MANY WAYS to approach Reacquaintance as there are couples. But common to every scenario are certain "musts"—necessary components of the process that will ensure that you get the most from Reacquaintance.

First Steps

The first step in Reacquaintance is to decide, as a couple, that you need to do something to bring yourselves closer together. This may take some discussion, particularly if one of you is hesitant. Don't be afraid to broach the subject to your partner; having the courage to say what you feel is key to Reacquaintance. And remember, your partner is the one person in the world you love more than any other, the person with whom you've been most intimate on any number of levels. Trust each other. And trust yourself—you can do it because this coming together, this closing up of the Intimacy Gap, is exactly the thing you've been hoping to do for so very long.

After you've both made a commitment to Reacquaintance—or even before you get to that stage—familiarize yourself with the chapters in the book, 1 and 2, that explain *why* most of us have lost touch with our mates. If you haven't already, both of you should read through the section on the research that's been done on this subject so that you understand how the Intimacy Gap opens up and how you can go about closing it. That way you'll have a better idea of what you're aiming for with Reacquaintance.

It's also important that you understand "The Ground Rules," the positions of Speaker and Listener, and the best methods of acting, reacting, and interacting during the process of Reacquaintance. Like all itineraries, it's meant to guide you through the best routes and help you make the most of your trip. But this is nothing if not a personal journey. Don't be afraid to venture off on your own if you feel the urge.

Beginning Your Reacquaintance: The First Morning

You've done the groundwork. You've read through this book, you've agreed to try Reacquaintance, you've cleared your schedules, and you've made arrangements for the kids, the pets, the newspaper, and the mail. You've decided on a setting and made the reservations. Now it's time to meet.

Before you begin your weekend, make two copies of "The Form for Reacquaintance" from the book, one for each of you. All of the answers should be written in pencil in case you have a change of mind, so make sure you pack a few, along with some good erasers and a couple of sharpeners.

As you discovered in chapter 3, you'll begin the experience separately, so you'll each need to find a place where you can fill out the Form privately, comfortably, and with no distractions. Maybe that's poolside at the hotel, or with a cup of tea on the veranda of the B and B. If you're at home, you can take the master bedroom and let your spouse have the family room. Just don't fill in the Forms together; you don't want anything but your inner voice to influence your answers.

Start at the beginning and move through each section in sequence. If you come to a topic that gives you pause, skip over it and return later. For specifics on how to word your answers, read through "The Ground Rules" on pages 41–42. And while you write, keep trusting that your partner loves you and wants to know all this about you.

We thought the Speaker/Listener procedure was great—which was terrific for me, by the way, because I seldom sit and listen. Reacquaintance probably wouldn't have been as successful for us otherwise, because we both tend to talk over each other so much.

—*Dick*

Afternoon of the First Day

It should take no more than two hours to fill out the Forms. Once you've finished, set them aside in a private place and forget about them for the rest of the afternoon. Don't discuss them. You both deserve a little time to decompress. Enjoy the rest of the day: Loll by the pool, take a nap, do a crossword puzzle together. Visit a museum, take a walk, windowshop, sightsee, go antiquing. Have a long lunch, alfresco, at a sidewalk café. Make love. Just be together.

Evening of the First Day

Here's when you discuss the Forms. This is the core of Reacquaintance, and it needs to be undertaken without interruption. If that's absolutely impossible, you can do it in two parts. But you'll get the most from it, emotionally and intellectually, if you can work through it in one sitting.

Just as you did when filling out the Forms, you should choose an environment that's comfortable and pleasing, this time to both of you. My wife and I, for example, have always enjoyed the experience over the course of a romantic dinner. If you opt for that, be sure to ask for a quiet table—away from the door, the kitchen, the wait station, or any heavily trafficked section of the room. And make sure it's the sort of place you can linger; the bum's rush will definitely take the luster off the Reacquaintance experience. If you're staying at a hotel, room service provides a wonderful alternative. Make sure the setting is suitably romantic: candlelight, flowers on the table, soft music in the background, and great food.

> I can't tell you how remarkable it made me feel. I got the sense that Dick was actually *listening* to me, that my thoughts and feelings actually *mattered* to him. This was a pretty radical change from how I used to feel before—I used to feel that he just went through the motions in the conversation, and that what I said really didn't register. It was like suddenly not being invisible anymore.
>
> —*Darlene*

Bed-and-breakfasts offer different possibilities: an afternoon in a garden gazebo, followed up with a nice dinner; an indoor picnic in front of the fireplace, if your room has one. If you've decided to take a cruise, consider your cabin if it's comfortable or choose a quiet section of the deck, before or after dinner. A spa stay lets you meet after a massage or steam bath, when you're feeling receptive and relaxed.

Wherever you've chosen to experience it, approach Reacquaintance with an open, enthusiastic mind, ready to spend an exciting evening with someone you love and who you know loves you.

The Ground Rules

Ideally, Reacquaintance should comprise an easy give-and-take of information and a fluid expression of honest emotions. Nevertheless, it's important that the process have a structure in which information and emotions can flow without friction. To this end, I offer the following guidelines.[1]

First, you need to acknowledge that you're both equals. In the arena of Reacquaintance, there's no room for power positions, no alpha person, no king or queen. You are two equal human beings. Neither you nor your partner is more important than the other, and neither of you has more, or less, at stake.

> I've always tended not to talk when I feel the most. Anger, anxiety, sorrow—they all just shut me down and shut me up. After Reacquaintance, though, I found that I was less likely to do that. I start to fall back into that old, silent pattern, and I stop myself now.
>
> —*Rob*

It's important to accept these premises because for the process to succeed, you need to be empathetic—capable of seeing, and accepting, the situation from your partner's point of view as well as your own. You want your partner to feel secure and safe, free of anxieties about losing your love or your respect or forfeiting the relationship altogether. Each of you has to feel certain that you and your viewpoints will be accepted without judgment.

To facilitate this, it's important that you follow a simple protocol when going through the Reacquaintance process: You'll be reading your answers to each topic in succession, first one of you, then the other. You can decide in advance who'll begin each topic—it's not necessary that the same person always begins or ends, and you can switch back and forth if you like. The person revealing their answer is the Speaker; the person hearing it is the Listener. Read through the following guide to each role; it's designed to help you and your partner communicate as freely as possible.

The Speaker

Just as you did when filling out the Form, you need to be honest and address the issue from your heart when you act as Speaker, resisting the urge to score emotional points. Be unafraid, trusting that your partner loves you and respects you and wants to know how your true self-of-the-moment feels about things.

In addition, you should:

- State your views subjectively. Your answers should be judgment-free, expressed strictly as your own perceptions. This keeps things uncharged and nonaggressive. Don't, for example, say, "We don't make love enough." This has more than a tinge of accusation in it or, at the least, a cold statement of fact, which could then be disputed by your partner if he or she feels threatened. It breeds defensiveness and distrust, which makes it hard for your partner to remain open and accepting about what you want your partner to understand. It makes him or her deal with the fact of *what* you said, rather than listening to what you're saying about yourself. Instead, phrase your answer as a personal feeling: "I'd like us to share lovemaking more often." There's no threat implied when you reveal your personal feelings, wants, or desires, only information about you and how you feel at the moment.

- Express your feelings whenever possible. You want your partner to know how you feel about things. Intellectual opinions are OK, but you relate to each other in the realm of feelings. So use them. Taking the above example of lovemaking, you could say, "I really like making love to you; I would like us to share that more often."

- Be specific. Avoid generalizations like, "I'd like to change careers," or, "I'm worried about our son." Instead, say, "I'd like to do social work because I want to touch other people's lives," or, "I'm concerned about the trouble Johnny's having in math; I'd like to find a way to improve his progress."

- Be positive. Positive energy begets positive energy, so let your partner see the positive side of you. Doing so may help disarm any potential reactions in emotionally charged areas. Taking the lovemaking example again, a more positive way to approach it might be, "You're a great lover. I really like making love with you. It makes me feel warm and safe and in touch with you. I would like us to share that more often."

- Stay away from "always" and "never." Absolutes leave no room for discussion. In the realm of relationships, things are rarely either "always" or "never," and overgeneralizations make it difficult for your partner to take you seriously and allow him or her to disagree with you or become defensive. Saying, for example, "We never make love anymore" makes it too easy for your partner to come back with a rebuttal, "Yes we do! We made love two months ago!" The object here is to let your partner know you'd like to be more intimate. Using trigger words like "always" and "never" clouds that simple message.

If you follow these guidelines, as you fill in your Form and as you read when Speaker, you'll minimize the possibility of confrontation, dispute, and wounded feelings.

The Listener

As important as the Speaker's role is to Reacquaintance—he or she is, after all, delivering the information that the process was created to elicit—it's the Listener who can make or break the experience. It's the Listener's display of respect, understanding, and acceptance that allows the Speaker to reveal him or herself freely and without fear.

As the Listener, you must:

- Respect the Speaker's moment. When the Speaker is talking—revealing his or her most authentic, innermost self, the Speaker has the floor. Give him or her the opportunity to speak *uninterrupted*, and allow the Speaker as much time as he or she needs to express his or her statements completely. The Listener should remain totally silent while the Speaker is revealing information about him or herself. This shows that you respect and value your partner and his or her viewpoints, and that it's important to you to hear what the Speaker has to say completely.

- *Really* listen. Put yourself in a receptive frame of mind and focus on what your partner is saying. Look at the Speaker and pay attention. Be empathetic—try to see things from the other's point of view, and do your best to set aside your own vision of the topic at hand. Concentrate, instead, on understanding *why* your partner is telling you what *he* or *she* thinks of something. This way, you help to create an atmosphere of acceptance that's so critical to the Reacquaintance experience.

- Don't question your partner's revelations. The Speaker needs to feel that he or she has total control over the communication of this personal information. While one of the great beauties of Reacquaintance is that it naturally creates conversation between partners, it's best not to ask questions that derail the Speaker's train of thought or force the Speaker to reveal information that your partner has chosen not to give at that particular moment. Questions like, "What makes you think that?" "How long have you felt this way?" "Have I done anything to make you feel this way?" can sound aggressive or defensive and destroy the sense of acceptance that the Listener must show to the Speaker for the process to work. It's equally important not to use a questioning tone of voice when you *do* respond to the Speaker—it puts your partner on the defensive and makes the Speaker feel he or she doesn't have control over the way information is revealed.

- Don't respond with your own opinion. When your partner has finished speaking on a particular topic, move on. Jumping in with your point of view is the perfect way to put your partner on the defensive or to tell him or her that you don't accept what your partner's just said. Be open. Put yourself in the Speaker's place and accept what he or she has to say without judgment. The Listener will eventually become the Speaker, and can use that time to voice his or her personal feelings about the subject under discussion. And if you really feel that a particular topic or response merits greater discussion, mark your Form and go back to discuss it after you've completed Reacquaintance.

- Don't interpret. Let the Speaker say what he or she has to say in their own way, from a personal perspective. Don't respond to a statement by restating it or trying to help the Speaker figure out why he or she feels the way they do. Resist the urge to psychoanalyze or to make connections between the information just revealed and anything else in the Speaker's life ("Don't you realize your mother always says the same thing?"). This effectively denies the validity of the revelation. It can make the Speaker feel inferior or send the message that you don't accept him or her. Let a Speaker's statement stand on its own.

- Don't make suggestions. The Listener isn't there to "fix" things for the Speaker—at least not during Reacquaintance. Solutions are for another time and place. For now, just listen, accept, and learn.

- *Don't make judgments!* This is by far the most important of the guidelines. Refrain from expressing your opinion on what you've just heard, verbally or through body language. It's hard not to mentally evaluate what you're hearing but try not to. At that moment, as the Listener, you're there only to listen and learn, to update what you know about this person you love. Your partner is telling you about him or herself, revealing what the Speaker knows and feels about his or her life. It's intensely personal, and at this moment, the Speaker is intensely vulnerable. So keep judgment out of the process.

Whichever role you're in—Speaker or Listener—it's of preeminent importance to show your respect for each other by listening and responding in a way that will build trust between you. Every time you offer your partner acceptance and understanding, you're reinforcing the sense that he or she can communicate more openly and honestly as the evening continues and, more importantly, as you live your lives together.

This is, of course, sometimes easier to say than to do. There may be moments during Reacquaintance when something your partner says about him or herself, you, or your life together will touch a nerve. Your first instinct will be to fire back at the Speaker, but again, you must work to suppress those basic instincts triggered by anger or hurt. They will only interfere with Reacquaintance and can damage the environment of safety and openness that you're trying to create. Take a long, slow, deep breath; hold it for a count of five; then let it out slowly. Break eye con-

tact for a moment; drop your head; close your eyes; and
concentrate on how your body feels. See if you can sense
where any tightness exists (I carry my tension across my
shoulders and neck). Tense those tight muscles, then let
them relax—feel them loosen a bit. Try to move your mind
off the emotion you're feeling and concentrate instead on
the fact that your partner is not trying to hurt you but is
only honestly expressing how he or she is feeling about
something. This is what the Speaker is supposed to be
doing; and while you may not care to hear it at the moment, do your best to accept what your partner has said as
his or her personal truth. This is what makes Reacquaintance work: openness, honesty, communication, and acceptance.

> During Reacquaintance, we did a cool thing we'd learned
> about in another workshop. We had what we called a "talk-
> ing stick," which we passed back and forth. Only the person
> in possession of the talking stick was allowed to speak. You
> can use anything you like for a "stick"—a stone, a candle—
> as long as it means a lot to both of you and you've imbued
> it with respect. If a couple is used to interrupting each
> other—as we were—it's particularly helpful.
>
> —*Karl*

Move through each topic in succession, one of you taking the role of Speaker, the other of Listener, then switch
roles for that topic. Once you've both spoken on a particular topic, you can, if you feel strongly about it, discuss it
briefly and nonjudgmentally—though I'd recommend sav-
ing an extended conversation on a specific topic for another
evening together. Then move on to the next topic. Take
as much time as you need. There's no reason to hurry, and
you've arranged things so that you have nothing else to do.

For me, one of the most important benefits of the Speaker/ Listener method was respect. By following the method closely, you suddenly find yourself respecting your mate more. I think there are times when people need to be granted respect rather than having to earn it. You can be completely worthy of respect, but if the other person isn't willing to give it to you, you don't feel it. But with the Speaker/Listener method, that respect is automatic, and suddenly you see that the other person deserves it.

—Nick

It's truly amazing how much you can communicate if you just have someone actively listening to you, totally focused on what you're saying.

—Andi

Don't be surprised if the process envelops you. You'll find yourself actually *looking* at your partner, in a way you haven't for a long time and *listening* intently to every revelation, *feeling* surprised and elated and proud and stimulated by what you hear. You'll be intrigued by this new-old person you love, and you'll be astonished by how much of your partner you thought you knew but didn't, by how much that was precious you've forgotten, by the degree to which your feelings for your partner have been glazed over by the day-to-day routine of relating to him or her. And your partner will feel exactly the same way about you.

After Reacquaintance, let the rest of the night take its course. Maybe you'll sit up talking into the wee hours, intrigued with and thrilled by this new person you've just met. Maybe you'll take a long, silent walk, hand-in-hand. Maybe you'll act on the passion of a refueled infatuation. Maybe you'll do and feel all of these things, maybe none of them.

Whatever the result of your Reacquaintance experience, just go with it. There's no right or wrong. However you end the evening, you'll come away knowing a great deal more about your friend and lover than you did when you began. And that's the whole point, isn't it?

The Second Day

As intense as it was, as thrilling and revelatory, everything you've done until now was essentially groundwork. You spent the first day and night of your forty-eight hours preparing and exploring, sharing and learning. Now it's time to reap the benefits. You're going to wake up today with a whole new vision of your partner and a desire to learn more. That is what this second day is for.

As you go through the day together, keep last night and its revelations fresh in your mind and make a conscious effort to see the new person your partner's become for you. This is extremely important because we all have a tendency to revert to old, familiar patterns. Keep on being the open, nonjudgmental, give-and-take person you became during Reacquaintance. Move and react to the new aspects of the person your partner has shown you. Pursue that new person.

Today, let the conversation flow; discuss whatever topic arises, including anything from the Form that particularly intrigued you. Fan the sparks of rekindled passion. Enjoy your partner—that suddenly "new" person you've been living with for so long. But don't let things stop there.

Use the knowledge you've gained during Reacquaintance. Now that you know more of your partner's hopes and desires, find out how you can help achieve them. Did you discover that your partner has always harbored a secret desire to paint? Drive to the mall that afternoon and stroll through an art store together. Offer creative assistance if you can: Suggest that you take the kids one or two nights a week so that he or she can sign up for an art class. Is your partner a skydiver wannabe? Pull out the phone book and look through it together, call a couple of jump schools, make a date to go to the school together (even though you, personally, would never think of flinging yourself from a perfectly good airplane). And let your partner do the same for you.

Above all, simply *be* together for this remaining time of your Reacquaintance weekend. Draw on what you learned as Speaker and Listener whenever you talk. Respect each other. Be empathetic. Speak subjectively and avoid all those trigger words. Above all, keep *listening*.

And when the forty-ninth hour begins, keep the last forty-eight in mind. Use what you've learned. Every day. Together.

6

THE FORM FOR REACQUAINTANCE

*I want to pretend I've just met you, love at first sight, and I
want to know who you are. I love you . . . but I don't know you.
And I want to know who this person is. . . .*
—AMY TAN, *THE BONESETTER'S DAUGHTER*

AS WE LEARNED IN CHAPTER 3, the catalyst of the Reacquaintance experience is "The Form for Reacquaintance."
I've included two copies of the Form in this chapter, one
for each of you. Feel free to pull them from the book,
though I would recommend simply making copies of them
so you can retain clean copies of the Form for future Reacquaintance experiences. I've also included a title and date
page on each Form so you can catalog your Forms over
time and refer back to them to see how your views of
yourselves and your lives have changed.

So now it begins. Enjoy yourselves. Enjoy each other.
Enjoy your Reacquaintance.

THE FORM FOR REACQUAINTANCE

Date:_____

PART ONE
M e

My three best attributes:
(What I like the most about me—my best characteristics and qualities.)

   1._____
   2._____
   3._____

My three worst attributes:
(The qualities or characteristics I think I need to work on.)

   1._____
   2._____
   3._____

On a scale of 1 to 10, when I think of my intelligence, I think I'm a:
(1 being the least intelligent, 10 being the most intelligent.)

   1._____

On a scale of 1 to 10, when I think of my attractiveness, I think I'm a:
(1 being the least attractive, 10 being the most attractive.)

   1._____

On a scale of 1 to 10, when I think of my social competence, I think I'm a:
(Think of social competence as how you interact with people in a social or public setting. In this sense, you would choose a lower number if you think you're too shy or intimidated in social situations or if you feel afraid that you're always about to make an embarrassing mistake. A 10 would mean you think you're the life of the party.)

1._____

On a scale of 1 to 10, when I think of my artistic abilities, I think I'm a:
(1 being not so artistic, 10 being very artistic. And this doesn't necessarily have to mean that you can or can't paint or sculpt or act. Your artistic sense can influence the way you decorate your house or lay out the garden.)

1._____

If I could change one thing about myself, it would be:
1._____

The part of my body I like the most:
1._____

The part of my body I like the least:
1._____

Two things that make me feel like I look great:
1._____
2._____

Two things that make me feel terrific about myself:
1._____
2._____

Two things that someone could do that would make me feel more terrific about myself:

    1._____
    2._____

Two things that make me feel cared about:

    1._____
    2._____

Two things I think people like about me:

    1._____
    2._____

Two things I think people overlook about me:

    1._____
    2._____

Two things I think people assume about me that aren't true:

    1._____
    2._____

My current biggest fear:

    1._____

My current biggest hope:

    1._____

Two things I feel I really need right now:

    1._____
    2._____

Two things I feel I really don't need right now:

    1._____
    2._____

My two main pet peeves:

   1._____

   2._____

My biggest worry about money is:

   1._____

The two things that relax me the most:

   1._____

   2._____

My worst habit:

   1._____

My best habit:

   1._____

The person who has influenced me most in my life:
(This could be a parent, a mentor, a friend, someone you met—
but give it some serious thought: Who in your life most influenced the direction your life has taken, is taking, or may take?)

   1._____

The historical figure I most identify with:
(What famous—or not so famous, as the case may be—person
do you feel you share traits or a life path with?)

   1._____

The living person I most admire:

   1._____

The two people I consider my greatest heroes in real life:

   1._____

   2._____

My greatest regrets:
   In the last year._____

   In my life._____

My greatest achievements:
   In the last year._____

   In my life._____

When and where I am the happiest:
(The time and place where all is right with the world—where you feel everything is just as it should be.)

   1._____

My most secret dream or desire at the moment:
(Something I really want—to own, to be, to do—that I haven't revealed until now.)

   1._____

PART TWO
What's Important to Me

My current primary priorities:
(The things I put first in my life—what's most important to me.)

1._____
2._____
3._____

My current secondary priorities:
(Things that are the next most important to me.)

1._____
2._____
3._____

My current tertiary priorities:
(Things I care a lot about but that aren't as important as the six things above.)

1._____
2._____
3._____

Three things I hope to accomplish/complete in the next three months:
(These can be from any part of your life—what goals, projects, or personal aspirations do you want to try to finish or achieve in the next ninety days?)

1._____
2._____
3._____

Three things I hope to accomplish/complete in the next six months:
(Again, what goals or projects would you like to achieve in the intermediate term?)

    1._____

    2._____

    3._____

Three things I hope to accomplish/complete in the next year:
(These are longer-term goals.)

    1._____

    2._____

    3._____

Something I'd like to accomplish before I die:
(Earn a doctorate? Paint a mural? Sing at Carnegie Hall? Travel around the world?)

    1._____

Three things I feel I could use my partner's help in accomplishing:
(They can be any of the things listed in the four questions above or something completely different.)

    1._____

    2._____

    3._____

Where I see myself in one, three, and five years:
(Consider what you'd like to be doing, how much money you'd like to be making, where you'd like to be living, what you'll look like, and so on.)

   1 year._____
   3 years._____
   5 years._____

Two things I think I'm really good at:
(This can be anything from work skills to specific sports or hobbies to social activities; they could include any talent, from public speaking to relating to children.)

   1._____
   2._____

Two things I wish I were better at:
(Things that I do now but want to be better at—work or social skills, specific sports, anything from any area of life.)

   1._____
   2._____

Two things I'd like to try artistically:
(Have you ever wanted to oil paint? Act? Sing? Sketch a nude? Write and direct a play?)

   1._____
   2._____

Two things I'd like to try athletically:
(Ever wanted to run a marathon? Fly a hot-air balloon? Be a pro football cheerleader/player/coach?)

   1._____
   2._____

Two things I'd like to try socially:
(Ever wanted to host a Sunday brunch? Throw a gala New Year's party? Attend an opera? Work at a charity or be on its board of directors?)

1._____

2._____

The thing I most value in a friend:
(Loyalty? Dependability? Accepting? Easy to get along with? The ability to listen?)

1._____

PART THREE
What I Do

The three things I most like about my current job:
  1._____
  2._____
  3._____

The three things I dislike most about my current job:
(Don't make this a bitching session. What really doesn't work for you?)

  1._____
  2._____
  3._____

Three things I would like to accomplish at work:
(These can be specific projects or goals or achievements, such as a promotion or an increase in salary.)

  1._____
  2._____
  3._____

My biggest problem at work right now:
(This can refer to yourself—for example, a lack of confidence or skills, or a bad attitude. Or it can be a problem with other workers or superiors. Again, don't make this a bitching session.)

  1._____

The kind of work I'd most like to do (other than what I do now):
  1._____

The kind of work I'd least like to do (other than what I do now):

1._____

Two things I think I can do but have never tried because I lacked knowledge or feared ridicule or failure:
(Think about those things in your work that you haven't tried because of the obstacles mentioned.)

1._____
2._____

Three things I would do if I had the time to devote to them:
(Things I currently don't do because of time limitations. These can be from any part of your life—work, play, social life, hobbies, charity, free time.)

1._____
2._____
3._____

Three things I would do if I had the money to do them:
(These can be simple things like repainting the house or extravagant things like taking a trip around the world. But make them things you'd *really* like to do not, just things that sound "neat.")

1._____
2._____
3._____

PART FOUR
What I Believe

The three defining concepts of my spiritual life at the moment:
(What do you believe? For example, do you believe in God? What type of God—benevolent, fatherly, vengeful? Does a specific organized religion play a big role in your life? Do you believe in a soul? Do you believe we're each here for a purpose? Do our ancestors watch over us? Is there an angel on your shoulder? Do you believe that prayer has power? In other words, do you think there's another side to life that affects our day-to-day actions? By the same token, if you have no beliefs concerning the spiritual side of life—that is, if you believe we only go around once, that this is it, that we're all basically just advanced forms of the mammal—then say so.)

1._____
2._____
3._____

Three philosophical ideas I align myself with at the moment:
(Different from religious or spiritual ideas, these are the rules we live our lives by—"Do unto others...," for instance, or the idea of predestination, or the concept of Karma: "if I steal this, something will be stolen from me later." What concepts make up your basic outlook on life?)

1._____
2._____
3._____

The greatest learning experience I've ever had:
(The time or incident that taught you the most about life and/or people—it can be a specific incident, or an experience like college, or a job, or an interaction with another person.)

1._____

A dream during sleep that I've recently had and what I think it means:

1._____

My best time of day:

1._____

PART FIVE
My Relationships

The person I consider to be my best friend:

1._____

The person I consider to be my best friend (other than my partner):
(Answer this one if your partner was your answer to the first statement.)

1._____

My best new friend is:
(Someone you've met recently whom you get along with well and would like to spend more time with.)

1._____

The person I feel most comfortable turning to when I really need to talk:
(This should be the person you don't feel you have to hold anything back from, whom you feel you can open up the most to.)

1._____

The three things I think define a healthy relationship:

1._____
2._____
3._____

The three things I feel define my role in our relationship:
(The things you feel you have responsibility for or that you provide in the relationship. For example: provider of money, manager of finances, primary caregiver for children. List these in order of importance.)

1._____
2._____
3._____

The three things I feel define my partner's role in our relationship:
(The things you feel your partner has responsibility for or provides in the partnership. Again, list these in order of importance.)

1._____
2._____
3._____

Two things about our relationship that I value the most:

1._____
2._____

Two things about our relationship that I would like to see further enhanced and developed:

1._____
2._____

The part of our relationship that I think could use a little attention:
(An area that you think needs some discussion; something that you've been meaning to bring up, but time and circumstances haven't allowed it. Remember, the time to discuss it is not necessarily now, but you want to define the area here.)

1._____
2._____

PART SIX
Intimacies

On a scale of I to 10, the importance I think intimacies like hugging, cuddling, and lovemaking have in a relationship:
(I being not important at all, 10 being most important.)

I._____

The number of times I'd like to make love in a week:
I._____

The two things I like most about lovemaking:
(This is totally subjective. Is it the physical feeling? Is it the closeness with someone? Is it getting lost from the world for a while? Is it the sense of being loved?)

I._____
2._____

My two current favorite places to make love:
(Indoors, outdoors? Bed, couch? In front of a fire?)

I._____
2._____

My current favorite time of day to make love:
I._____

My three favorite foreplay things *to do* to my partner:
(What gives you the most pleasure while giving your partner pleasure? Lovemaking is as much about giving as receiving. Let your partner know what *you* like to *do*.)

I._____
2._____
3._____

My three favorite foreplay things *to have done to me* by my partner:

(The flip side of the coin. What really gets *you* going? What things does your partner do that *you* like the most?)

1._____

2._____

3._____

Two lovemaking positions I would like to try:

(Over time, we may tend to fall into a habitual way of doing things. Sometimes it just takes a little conscious thought to respark some excitement.)

1._____

2._____

An erotic fantasy I feel comfortable sharing:

(The key word here is "comfortable." We all have fantasies. But they reside in our most protected and secret selves and sharing them requires us to become vulnerable in that area. There's nothing wrong with wanting to keep this area totally private. If you're not comfortable delving into it, skip this topic.)

1._____

My idea of a romantic evening would be:

(A phone call from work asking to meet for drinks and dinner? Flowers? Dinner by candlelight? A warm blanket in front of a blazing fire? Sending the kids to Grandma's for the night? Walking hand in hand on the beach at midnight? Write out the entire story if you like.)

1. _____
_____
_____
_____
_____
_____
_____
_____

PART SEVEN
Home and Family

Three things I really like about our home:

    1._____

    2._____

    3._____

Three things I'd like to change about our home:
(Things you'd like to redecorate, or rebuild, remove, or add.)

    1._____

    2._____

    3._____

My least favorite household obligation (or chore) is:

    1._____

Two things that make me happiest about our family:

    1._____

    2._____

Three strengths I think our family has:
(Is it how you all pull for each other? The balance of power? The
cooperation? A grounding in religion? Openness? Respect across
generational lines?)

    1._____

    2._____

    3._____

Three areas I think our family needs work on:
(Communication? Tolerance? Compassion? Doing things together?)

    1._____

    2._____

    3._____

My two favorite meals (that we make at home):

    1._____

    2._____

My two favorite meals (that I've had in a restaurant):
(These can be single meals that have stood out among many and that you'd like to have again or specific dishes that you keep going back for.)

    1._____

    2._____

My favorite restaurant:

    1._____

My current three favorite types of entertainment:

    1._____

    2._____

    3._____

My two favorite things to do with friends:

    1._____

    2._____

My two favorite things to do with the kids:

    1._____

    2._____

The place I'd like to go for my next vacation:
(Where would you *really* like to go, regardless of cost or other practicalities?)

1._____

The two things I like most about my partner:
(Dedication to work or family? Sense of humor? Smile? Physical attributes?)

1._____
2._____

The two things that make me proudest of my partner:
(How hard he works? Her selflessness? His persistence in getting things accomplished? Her character under pressure? His tenderness with the children?)

1._____
2._____

What makes me proudest of my children:
(Answer this in two ways: First, what makes you proudest of the kids overall? Second, what about each child makes you proudest?)

Overall._____
Child 1._____
Child 2._____
Child 3._____
Child 4._____

My biggest worries about my children:
(Again, answer in two ways: overall and individually.)

Overall._____
Child 1._____
Child 2._____
Child 3._____
Child 4._____

The thing I find most difficult about being a parent:
1._____

The most important thing I think we as parents should give our children:
1._____

PART EIGHT
Things Specific to Us

This section is where you can begin to add topics that are specific to you and your partner—things that occur to you throughout the experience of Reacquaintance that you'd like to know about your partner or share about yourself. Don't limit yourself—there are no boundaries—and let this section grow with you through the years of continual Reacquaintance.

THE FORM FOR REACQUAINTANCE

Date:_____

PART ONE
Me

My three best attributes:
(What I like the most about me—my best characteristics and qualities.)

1._____
2._____
3._____

My three worst attributes:
(The qualities or characteristics I think I need to work on.)

1._____
2._____
3._____

On a scale of 1 to 10, when I think of my intelligence, I think I'm a:
(1 being the least intelligent, 10 being the most intelligent.)

1._____

On a scale of 1 to 10, when I think of my attractiveness, I think I'm a:
(1 being the least attractive, 10 being the most attractive.)

1._____

On a scale of 1 to 10, when I think of my social competence, I think I'm a:
(Think of social competence as how you interact with people in a social or public setting. In this sense, you would choose a lower number if you think you're too shy or intimidated in social situations, or if you feel afraid that you're always about to make an embarrassing mistake. A 10 would mean you think you're the life of the party.)

1._____

On a scale of 1 to 10, when I think of my artistic abilities, I think I'm a:
(1 being not so artistic, 10 being very artistic. And this doesn't necessarily have to mean that you can or can't paint or sculpt or act. Your artistic sense can influence the way you decorate your house or lay out the garden.)

1._____

If I could change one thing about myself, it would be:
1._____

The part of my body I like the most:
1._____

The part of my body I like the least:
1._____

Two things that make me feel like I look great:
1._____
2._____

Two things that make me feel terrific about myself:
1._____
2._____

Two things that someone could do that would make me feel more terrific about myself:

1._____

2._____

Two things that make me feel cared about:

1._____

2._____

Two things I think people like about me:

1._____

2._____

Two things I think people overlook about me:

1._____

2._____

Two things I think people assume about me that aren't true:

1._____

2._____

My current biggest fear:

1._____

My current biggest hope:

1._____

Two things I feel I really need right now:

1._____

2._____

Two things I feel I really don't need right now:

1._____

2._____

My two main pet peeves:

 1._____

 2._____

My biggest worry about money is:

 1._____

The two things that relax me the most:

 1._____

 2._____

My worst habit:

 1._____

My best habit:

 1._____

The person who has influenced me most in my life:
(This could be a parent, a mentor, a friend, someone you met—
but give it some serious thought: Who in your life most influenced the direction your life has taken, is taking, or may take?)

 1._____

The historical figure I most identify with:
(What famous—or not so famous, as the case may be—person
do you feel you share traits or a life path with?)

 1._____

The living person I most admire:

 1._____

The two people I consider my greatest heroes in real life:

 1._____

 2._____

My greatest regrets:
　　In the last year._____
　　In my life._____

My greatest achievements:
　　In the last year._____
　　In my life._____

When and where I am the happiest:
(The time and place where all is right with the world—where you feel everything is just as it should be.)

　　I._____

My most secret dream or desire at the moment:
(Something I really want—to own, to be, to do—that I haven't revealed until now.)

　　I._____

PART TWO
What's Important to Me

My current primary priorities:
(The things I put first in my life—what's most important to me.)

1._____
2._____
3._____

My current secondary priorities:
(Things that are the next most important to me.)

1._____
2._____
3._____

My current tertiary priorities:
(Things I care a lot about but that aren't as important as the six things above.)

1._____
2._____
3._____

Three things I hope to accomplish/complete in the next three months:
(These can be from any part of your life—what goals, projects, or personal aspirations do you want to try to finish or achieve in the next ninety days?)

1._____
2._____
3._____

Three things I hope to accomplish/complete in the next six months:

(Again, what goals or projects would you like to achieve in the intermediate term?)

    1._____
    2._____
    3._____

Three things I hope to accomplish/complete in the next year:

(These are longer-term goals.)

    1._____
    2._____
    3._____

Something I'd like to accomplish before I die:

(Earn a doctorate? Paint a mural? Sing at Carnegie Hall? Travel around the world?)

    1._____

Three things I feel I could use my partner's help in accomplishing:

(They can be any of the things listed in the four questions above or something completely different.)

    1._____
    2._____
    3._____

Where I see myself in one, three, and five years:

(Consider what you'd like to be doing, how much money you'd like to be making, where you'd like to be living, what you'll look like, and so on.)

I year._____
3 years._____
5 years._____

Two things I think I'm really good at:

(This can be anything from work skills to specific sports or hobbies to social activities; they could include any talent, from public speaking to relating to children.)

1._____
2._____

Two things I wish I were better at:

(Things that I do now but want to be better at—work or social skills, specific sports, anything from any area of life.)

1._____
2._____

Two things I'd like to try artistically:

(Have you ever wanted to oil paint? Act? Sing? Sketch a nude? Write and direct a play?)

1._____
2._____

Two things I'd like to try athletically:

(Ever wanted to run a marathon? Fly a hot-air balloon? Be a pro football cheerleader/player/coach?)

1._____
2._____

Two things I'd like to try socially:

(Ever wanted to host a Sunday brunch? Throw a gala New Year's party? Attend an opera? Work at a charity or be on its board of directors?)

1._____

2._____

The thing I most value in a friend:

(Loyalty? Dependability? Accepting? Easy to get along with? The ability to listen?)

1._____

PART THREE
What I Do

The three things I most like about my current job:

1._____
2._____
3._____

The three things I dislike most about my current job:
(Don't make this a bitching session. What really doesn't work for you?)

1._____
2._____
3._____

Three things I would like to accomplish at work:
(These can be specific projects or goals or achievements, such as a promotion or an increase in salary.)

1._____
2._____
3._____

My biggest problem at work right now:
(This can refer to yourself—for example, a lack of confidence or skills, or a bad attitude. Or it can be a problem with other workers or superiors. Again, don't make this a bitching session.)

1._____

The kind of work I'd most like to do (other than what I do now):

1._____

The kind of work I'd least like to do (other than what I do now):

   1._____

Two things I think I can do but have never tried because I lacked knowledge or feared ridicule or failure:

(Think about those things in your work that you haven't tried because of the obstacles mentioned.)

   1._____
   2._____

Three things I would do if I had the time to devote to them:

(Things I currently don't do because of time limitations. These can be from any part of your life—work, play, social life, hobbies, charity, free time.)

   1._____
   2._____
   3._____

Three things I would do if I had the money to do them:

(These can be simple things like repainting the house or extravagant things like taking a trip around the world. But make them things you'd *really* like to do, not just things that sound "neat.")

   1._____
   2._____
   3._____

PART FOUR
What I Believe

The three defining concepts of my spiritual life at the moment:
(What do you believe? For example, do you believe in God? What type of God—benevolent, fatherly, vengeful? Does a specific organized religion play a big role in your life? Do you believe in a soul? Do you believe we're each here for a purpose? Do our ancestors watch over us? Is there an angel on your shoulder? Do you believe that prayer has power? In other words, do you think there's another side to life that affects our day-to-day actions? By the same token, if you have no beliefs concerning the spiritual side of life—that is, if you believe we only go around once, that this is it, that we're all basically just advanced forms of the mammal—then say so.)

1._____
2._____
3._____

Three philosophical ideas I align myself with at the moment:
(Different from religious or spiritual ideas, these are the rules we live our lives by—"Do unto others...," for instance, or the idea of predestination, or the concept of Karma: "if I steal this, something will be stolen from me later." What concepts make up your basic outlook on life?)

1._____
2._____
3._____

The greatest learning experience I've ever had:
(The time or incident that taught you the most about life and/or people—it can be a specific incident, or an experience like college, or a job, or an interaction with another person.)

1._____

A dream during sleep that I've recently had and what I think it means:

1._____

My best time of day:

1._____

PART FIVE
My Relationships

The person I consider to be my best friend:
   1._____

The person I consider to be my best friend (other than my partner):
(Answer this one if your partner was your answer to the first statement.)

   1._____

My best new friend is:
(Someone you've met recently whom you get along with well and would like to spend more time with.)

   1._____

The person I feel most comfortable turning to when I really need to talk:
(This should be the person you don't feel you have to hold anything back from, whom you feel you can open up the most to.)

   1._____

The three things I think define a healthy relationship:
   1._____
   2._____
   3._____

The three things I feel define my role in our relationship:
(The things you feel you have responsibility for or that you provide in the relationship. For example: provider of money, manager of finances, primary caregiver for children. List these in order of importance.)

1._____
2._____
3._____

The three things I feel define my partner's role in our relationship:
(The things you feel your partner has responsibility for or provides in the partnership. Again, list these in order of importance.)

1._____
2._____
3._____

Two things about our relationship that I value the most:

1._____
2._____

Two things about our relationship that I would like to see further enhanced and developed:

1._____
2._____

The part of our relationship that I think could use a little attention:
(An area that you think needs some discussion; something that you've been meaning to bring up, but time and circumstances haven't allowed it. Remember, the time to discuss it is not necessarily now, but you want to define the area here.)

1._____
2._____

PART SIX
Intimacies

On a scale of 1 to 10, the importance I think intimacies like hugging, cuddling, and lovemaking have in a relationship:
(1 being not important at all, 10 being most important.)

1._____

The number of times I'd like to make love in a week:

1._____

The two things I like most about lovemaking:
(This is totally subjective. Is it the physical feeling? Is it the closeness with someone? Is it getting lost from the world for a while? Is it the sense of being loved?)

1._____
2._____

My two current favorite places to make love:
(Indoors, outdoors? Bed, couch? In front of a fire?)

1._____
2._____

My current favorite time of day to make love:

1._____

My three favorite foreplay things *to do* to my partner:
(What gives you the most pleasure while giving your partner pleasure? Lovemaking is as much about giving as receiving. Let your partner know what *you* like to *do*.)

1._____
2._____
3._____

My three favorite foreplay things *to have done to me* by my partner:
(The flip side of the coin. What really gets *you* going? What things does your partner do that *you* like the most?)

1._____
2._____
3._____

Two lovemaking positions I would like to try:
(Over time, we may tend to fall into a habitual way of doing things. Sometimes it just takes a little conscious thought to respark some excitement.)

1._____
2._____

An erotic fantasy I feel comfortable sharing:
(The key word here is "comfortable." We all have fantasies. But they reside in our most protected and secret selves and sharing them requires us to become vulnerable in that area. There's nothing wrong with wanting to keep this area totally private. If you're not comfortable delving into it, skip this topic.)

1._____

My idea of a romantic evening would be:

(A phone call from work asking to meet for drinks and dinner? Flowers? Dinner by candlelight? A warm blanket in front of a blazing fire? Sending the kids to Grandma's for the night? Walking hand in hand on the beach at midnight? Write out the entire story if you like.)

1._____
_____
_____
_____
_____
_____
_____
_____

PART SEVEN
Home and Family

Three things I really like about our home:

1._____
2._____
3._____

Three things I'd like to change about our home:
(Things you'd like to redecorate, or rebuild, remove, or add.)

1._____
2._____
3._____

My least favorite household obligation (or chore) is:

1._____

Two things that make me happiest about our family:

1._____
2._____

Three strengths I think our family has:
(Is it how you all pull for each other? The balance of power? The cooperation? A grounding in religion? Openness? Respect across generational lines?)

1._____
2._____
3._____

Three areas I think our family needs work on:
(Communication? Tolerance? Compassion? Doing things together?)

   1._____

   2._____

   3._____

My two favorite meals (that we make at home):

   1._____

   2._____

My two favorite meals (that I've had in a restaurant):
(These can be single meals that have stood out among many and that you'd like to have again or specific dishes that you keep going back for.)

   1._____

   2._____

My favorite restaurant:

   1._____

My current three favorite types of entertainment:

   1._____

   2._____

   3._____

My two favorite things to do with friends:

   1._____

   2._____

My two favorite things to do with the kids:

   1._____

   2._____

The place I'd like to go for my next vacation:
(Where would you *really* like to go, regardless of cost or other practicalities?)

    I._____

The two things I like most about my partner:
(Dedication to work or family? Sense of humor? Smile? Physical attributes?)

    I._____
    2._____

The two things that make me proudest of my partner:
(How hard he works? Her selflessness? His persistence in getting things accomplished? Her character under pressure? His tenderness with the children?)

    I._____
    2._____

What makes me proudest of my children:
(Answer this is two ways: First, what makes you proudest of the kids overall? Second, what about each child makes you proudest?)

    Overall._____
    Child I._____
    Child 2._____
    Child 3._____
    Child 4._____

My biggest worries about my children:
(Again, answer in two ways: overall and individually.)

    Overall._____

    Child 1._____

    Child 2._____

    Child 3._____

    Child 4._____

The thing I find most difficult about being a parent:

    1._____

The most important thing I think we as parents should give our children:

    1._____

PART EIGHT
Things Specific to Us

This section is where you can begin to add topics that are specific to you and your partner—things that occur to you throughout the experience of Reacquaintance that you'd like to know about your partner or share about yourself. Don't limit yourself—there are no boundaries—and let this section grow with you through the years of continual Reacquaintance.

7

LIVING WHAT YOU'VE LEARNED

Forward, forward, let us range,
Let the great world spin for ever down the ringing
grooves of change.
—ALFRED, LORD TENNYSON, "THE LORD OF BURLEIGH"

FOR MOST COUPLES, THE END RESULT of Reacquaintance is an enhanced sense of understanding and acceptance and a deepening of the bond that drew them together in the first place. Nevertheless, Reacquaintance isn't an end in itself. During the process, each partner will be amassing an enormous amount of new information about the other—an extraordinary, revelatory experience in and of itself. But far more important than the experience itself and the insight it offers is the way each of you chooses to use that information over time.

The "Intimacies" section was the most profound for me. Boy, when we got to the fantasies part—that was great for me. Although you think you know what pleases your partner, hearing ideas about how to create a new setting or being told, "Hey, this is what I'd like to try"—it's an eye-opener. Both of us really liked that part, and we've liked what's happened since then because of it.

—*Liz*

Keeping the Connection

As you learned in chapter 5, Reacquaintance can help you take a more active role in your partner's life. You can do this daily in a multitude of ways—by offering encouragement, support, and inspiration; by being tolerant, open-minded, and cooperative; by taking the time for romance; by risking your own comfort and vulnerability.

Think, for example, what might happen if you encouraged your partner to finish the courses needed to complete that degree and overcome the sense of regret that's lingered for so many years. What would it take? An offer to watch the kids and do the housework a few nights a week? Some rejuggling of the family budget? Or imagine the joy you could spark by surprising your mate with the tools he or she needs to try that long-thought-about hobby? And what if you took an interest in that hobby yourself? Perhaps you could take the time to help him or her study for the exam your partner will need to get that promotion he or she wants to go after. And how easily could you validate your partner's spirit by setting aside your own beliefs for a while and agreeing to open-mindedly visit that new church he or she expressed an interest in?

> Out of everything Beth revealed, the revelation that hit me hardest was the fact that her sister was the person she felt most comfortable confiding in. That should have been me. And now I'm working hard to make it me.
>
> —*Rob*

For many couples, Reacquaintance offers new opportunities to spend more time together. Maybe you've discovered that you both want to learn to play bridge or take a martial arts course or enroll in the local cooking school or try out for a play at the community theater. Maybe you've never given ballroom dancing a thought in your life—but when your spouse said he or she had always hankered to learn, it suddenly sounded good to you.

> I think the most immediate result of Reacquaintance was that I got flowers sent to me the very next day. Do you know how long it's been since I got flowers? Wow!
>
> —*Liz*

Use what you've learned to enhance your family life as well. Maybe your spouse would love to see you more involved with the kids. Make the time for it. Help with the homework. Watch a kids' video. Play a little Nintendo. Fly a kite. And how about that dream vacation he or she told you about? Why couldn't you help make it a reality? Plan it together: Bring home some brochures, do an Internet search, stop by a travel agency. If what your partner wants is simply more of you in his or her life, consider that you may have been working too much or focusing too much on things outside the home. Reacquaintance can be a powerful wake-up call.

Allow the art of conversation to make a comeback in your relationship. You have new subjects to explore now, new topics to discuss. Turn off the TV one or two nights a week and just talk. Choose a subject and explore it together, much as you did during Reacquaintance.

And don't overlook the little things your partner revealed—sometimes they're more important than all those so-called matters of substance. Does she love flowers? Send her some. Does he think showering together is sexy? Indulge him. Does she want you to speak more tenderly to her? You can do it. If she mentioned she'd like to try starting a vegetable garden, get her a gardening book. Create your spouse's "idea for a romantic evening" down to the smallest detail—become the romantic rogue or ingenue you know you can be or, more importantly, that *your spouse thinks you can be*. Look through your partner's "Form for Reacquaintance" a second time. Remind yourself of the seemingly inconsequential things—they were important enough for your partner to write down, weren't they? Pay attention to them. Deliver on those dreams and hopes without being asked to.

> I came away from our Reacquaintance really being *in love* again. I would never have believed it, but that's what it felt like. It put us so closely in touch with each other again, made us really *feel* each other again.
>
> —*Nick*

What does all this boil down to? Giving more of your time and yourself. That, after all, is at the heart of what impelled you to consider Reacquaintance in the first place.

Now you have some concrete, insightful ideas of how to do it.

Above all, use the tools that you've learned. Remember the roles of Speaker and Listener and the simple Ground Rules that govern them and apply them every time you speak with your partner. When you get home in the evening, instead of rushing through a *Reader's Digest* version of your day, take the time to sit down, decompress, look at each other, and offer some genuine conversation. It doesn't have to take hours; ten minutes of focused, involved, caring communication is worth a day of mindless chatter disguising itself as conversation.

Become *especially* aware of those times you'd be better off as Listener. Though we usually think otherwise, listening is the heart and soul of real communication. And when you're finished listening, respond with empathy and understanding.

The concepts that inform the roles of Speaker and Listener can be applied in every facet of your life and every conversation you have—at home, at work, in social situations. The true conversationalist is a well-schooled listener. And you've just graduated.

When we agreed to go through Reacquaintance, I think what I really wanted was to find the old Rob—the Rob I'd fallen in love with two decades ago. That didn't happen because of course the old Rob was somebody I'd made up. I'd imagined him. But here's the great thing: The new Rob—the person I met during Reacquaintance—turns out to be so much more interesting.

—Beth

Hello Again—and Again

Finally, make sure you stay reacquainted. Change isn't going to slow down or stop happening, in you or your partner. In fact, Reacquaintance itself is an engine for change, and you'll need to find a way to keep up with it.

There are lots of ways to do this. You might, for instance, schedule mini-Reacquaintances on a monthly or bimonthly basis. Take one topic and delve into it deeply. Spend several days beforehand turning it over in your mind. Set out questions that you'd like to discuss with your partner. Then plan a night out or an afternoon alone together.

On the other hand, you might want to go through an abbreviated process of Reacquaintance weekly, maybe on Friday night or Saturday morning. Use the time to catch each other up on what's happened with you during the previous week. If you're anything like my wife, Toni, and me, you simply don't have enough time during the week to discuss in depth everything that's happened to you, let alone what's going on in your heart and your mind. With a little effort, you can create a shortened version of "The Form for Reacquaintance" covering the main facets of your life—personal concerns, work, spiritual and philosophical matters, relationships, and home life—and use it to update yourselves on a weekly basis.

However you employ it in the short-term, I highly recommend that you make an annual event of the full forty-eight-hour Reacquaintance. No matter how effectively the two of you stay in touch and informed, there's no substitute for the intimacy and focus that a Reacquaintance retreat can provide. First and foremost, you'll be alone together. You can forget about responsibilities, take a deep breath, and slow down the world. You can take time to hold each other, body and soul. You can step back and see yourself and each other clearly, without any of the static of

> I can't express how valuable I think the experience of Reacquaintance can be to a relationship. I think it's been *very* important to us in that it identified and headed off a serious problem between us. People should be told that they are going to, *very definitely,* find themselves drawn closer to their mate, with more understanding of them. It is a remarkable experience and one you can't afford not to have with the one you love.
>
> —*Dick*

everyday life obscuring the picture. More important, you can see where you've been—and maybe where you're going. By comparing your current responses on the Form with the ones you made on a previous Reacquaintance, you can get an idea of patterns and trends, of growth and maturity, of direction and achievement.

Looking at Reacquaintance over time is a bit like seeing in three dimensions when you've gotten used to staring at a flat screen. You begin to see change itself and to embrace it instead of fear it. You start to understand what change really is—it's life, plain and simple. And you begin to recognize that life force in yourself, in your partner, and in your relationship.

Enjoy every second of it.

> This is the bottom line for me: If your relationship could use a real boost, if you think you're losing touch, if you want a great experience that will resonate through your entire life, both individually and as a couple, then get Reacquainted. Just do it. You have no idea how much you're missing.
>
> —*Nick*

ENDNOTES

Chapter 2: Do I Really Know What I Think I Know?
1. They published the results of their study in the *Journal of Personality and Social Psychology* 73, no. 4 (1997): 747–57.
2. Swann Jr., William B., and Michael J. Gill. "Confidence and Accuracy in Person Perception: Do We Know What We Think We Know About Our Relationship Partners?" *Journal of Personality and Social Psychology* 73, no. 4 (1997): 747–57.
3. Ibid.
4. Ibid.

Chapter 5: The Method
1. I have based these guidelines on the theories and techniques developed by Bernard G. Guerney Jr., a pioneering relationship psychologist. His book, *Relationship Enhancement* (San Francisco: Jossey-Bass Publishers, 1977), is a remarkable teaching text for professional couples counselors. If you would like to read more about communications techniques between relationship partners, I highly recommend this book.